I Am Still Your Negro

UNIVERSITY *of* **ALBERTA** PRESS

Valerie Mason-John

I Am Still Your Negro

An Homage to James Baldwin

Published by

University of Alberta Press
1–16 Rutherford Library South
11204 89 Avenue NW
Edmonton, Alberta, Canada T6G 2J4
uap.ualberta.ca

LIBRARY AND ARCHIVES CANADA
CATALOGUING IN PUBLICATION

Title: I am still your negro : an homage to
    James Baldwin / Valerie Mason-John.
Names: Mason-John, Valerie, author.
Series: Robert Kroetsch series.
Description: Series statement: Robert
    Kroetsch series | Poems.
Identifiers: Canadiana (print) 20190208805 |
    Canadiana (ebook) 2019020883X |
    ISBN 9781772125108 (softcover) |
    ISBN 9781772125191 (PDF)
Classification: LCC PS8626.A79868 I2 2020 |
    DDC C811/.6—dc23

First edition, first printing, 2020.

Editing and proofreading by
Jannie Edwards.

A volume in the Robert Kroetsch Series.

University of Alberta Press is committed to
protecting our natural environment.

University of Alberta Press gratefully
acknowledges the support received for its
publishing program from the Government
of Canada, the Canada Council for the Arts,
and the Government of Alberta through the
Alberta Media Fund.

Every effort has been made to identify
copyright holders and obtain permission for
the use of copyright material. Please notify
University of Alberta Press of any additions
or corrections that should be incorporated
in future reprints or editions of this book.

For my Black Afro-Diasporic communities scattered throughout the universe: May we all find liberation; may we free ourselves from the epigenetic chains of slavery.

I am still your negro

AND

I am not your negro

Contents

IX *Foreword* GEORGE ELLIOTT CLARKE

XIII *ID*

XVII *Introduction*

#Undocumented

2 Back a Yard

4 My Father's Prayer

5 Sticks and Stones

#ThisIsAfricanDiaspora

8 Yaata's Lament

11 The Ghost of Thomas Peters

17 I Am Africa

20 African Feet

22 The Windrush

25 I Am Still Your Negro

28 Another One Bites the Dust

#MeToo

30 Yaata's Yowl

32 Business

33 Golden Virginia

34 The Villain

36 The Perfect Road

38 The Couplet

40 #MeToo

48 Playing Dead

#IfMyPlantsCouldSpeak

50   Yaata's Groan

53   Yellowknife

56   The Binge

57   The VindaLoo

58   Anorectic

#Swag

60   Yaata's Manifesto

63   The Front Line

64   Sixty Seconds

65   Stalk Time

68   Mothercare

#RaveScene

70   Yaata's Rap

71   Essentials for Heaven

72   Cinders Time

76   My First Half

80   Class A

#Intersectionality

82   Yaata's Prophecy

84   Self Portrait 1: The Colour of My Skin

85   Self Portrait 2: Call Me My Name

87   Man-ifestation

89   A Wake

91   Forget and Pretend

93   Again Becoming

94   Farewell My Fiend

95   **Yaata's Epilogue**

97   *Acknowledgements*

Foreword

On the Righteous, Right-On, Diasporic Diatribe of our Tribe: Introducing Our Unstill, "Negro" Poet, Valerie Mason-John, a.k.a. "Queenie"

ACCORDIN TO GENESIS, God commissioned Adam to help start off Creation by givin every critter a name. There's something to that: The cataloguing of creatures, places, things; branding the incarnate and the carnal with a searing denotation as good as a definition, and then needing poets to revise or overthrow what was given. I go back to Genesis in contemplating this book, this "homage to James Baldwin," and the titular adaptation of the screenplay title, *I Am Not Your Negro*, by noting that the author of *I Am Still Your Negro* bears a name that, from first to last (just like my own), echoes Anglo imperialism. Yet, Valerie Mason-John is also, in her stage name, the inversion of Her Royal Britannic (Satanic) Majesty. As Queenie—the egalitarian poet— righteous, sassy, interrogative, expletive-undeleted, rhetorical, and dynamic, it's her mission to re-brand African Diasporic history, not as the "civilizing triumph" of Caucasian, Christian, capitalist imperialists, but rather as the saga of survival of the Fanonian "wretched of the Earth" versus the warmongering and super-profitable (and environmentally destructive) ways (rapes and ravages) of White Supremacy. In this sense, she voices the diatribe of the Afro-Diasporic "tribe." She resists the names handed down to her, and speaks Truth to power as Queenie, as a proud, Black African woman, as a proud Queer sister, as a Sierra-Leonean-Canadian, connecting, in her very DNA, the often repressed, historical connection between Nova Scotia and

Sierra Leone. Thus, Queenie reminds me of the similar poetic, similar sonorous and strident power of Lemuel Johnson and Syl Cheney-Coker, also poets, also Sierra Leonean, who also spit fire back at the Empire that enslaved, exploited, and brutalized our ancestors—on both sides of the Atlantic (not to mention in Oceania—Australia, Papua New Guinea, New Zealand). She has seized command of the anti-colonial, Africanist canon, to rub folks' noses right in the offal—the awful—of a history that isn't even history yet, but still resonant in today's headlines.

Queenie tells it like it is about ourselves: "I descend from slaves on both sides of my family. I am proud to call myself a Creole from Sierra Leone." Yes, there is that African record—chronicle—awash in blood loosed by shark and whip and gun; in tears triggered by children sold off, raped, murdered; in the sweat that mined and farmed and built and worked, handing centuries of power and planetary riches to Europe that, thus empowered, found it necessary to compose operas and encyclopedias and hymns, all dedicated to the evil and backward idea that we "Negroes" are inferior. Queenie riffles the history tomes and newspapers to disgorge the crimes of slavery, of racism, of segregation, of genocide. She appeals to a Goddess, Yaata, to be her Muse and help her bear witness: To "The backbone of my people broken to smithereens"; to ancestors, "Shackled neck to neck / Clamped foot to foot / Frog-marched to Bunce Island ... / Sold for a bottle of rum / And a pouch of tobacco"; to Africa, "Birthing the first humanoid"; to Trump's America, making me "a Nigger Again." The writing is fierce; the voice is strong; the attitude is intimidating. Who can speak back against Queenie's speaking back? Dare ya try!

But racism isn't her only *bête blanche* (to coin a phrase), so are sexism and homophobia. Queenie spells out—with undeniable fact and antipathy to tact—the oppression of women, of Lesbians, and the steady warfare against mothers and daughters and aunts and sisters and lovers and spouses that's signified by the fact that half of us humans–i.e., women—own but a smidgen of its property and wealth.

And she's self-critical, too, which is just what we need in a prophet—like Malcolm X—who can speak to our frailties because he suffers em too. So, Queenie's gone to those raves, done the drugs, acted foolishly (hear that phrase from Al Green, here, from "Call Me"); she knows that too many of us think that "Essentials for Heaven" include "Facebook ... / Snapchat / WhatsApp / Netflix // Sleeping Pill" For me, *I Am Still Your Negro* applies to the page what The Last Poets put down on vinyl half-a-century back: The loud, awesome *Truth*, folks, whether ya like it or not!

GEORGE ELLIOTT CLARKE

7th Parliamentary (Canadian) Poet Laureate (2016–17)

ID

I DESCEND FROM SLAVES on both sides of my family. I am proud to call myself a Creole from Sierra Leone. My existence is proof of my intergenerational strength and epigenetic wisdom, despite the fact that my last name bears the memory of the trauma of my ancestry. I am a stateless Indigenous person.

I was born in England and raised in orphanages and foster homes with white carers and in white English environments. And so, at times, my mind is mixed race. Therefore, I feel at home borrowing from many cultures to tell my stories.

Now an African Canadian, I straddle the historical connections of Nova Scotia and Sierra Leone and I am working on piecing together much of this history, largely unknown in the rest of the world. My social services documents record the name Joseph McCarthy as my father, a name that was known in Nova Scotia during the 1800s. Many of these McCarthys repatriated back to Sierra Leone. Who knows, I could come from this lineage.

I was first inspired to write by E. M. Forster's *A Passage to India*, many years ago. I still remember the significance of the Bridge Party, an attempt to bridge two cultures that went horribly wrong. I have been trying to bridge cultures, genders, sexualities, all my life. Being Black and transracially raised, labelled cisgender female at birth, and now able to embrace the spectrum of gender fluidity, I have had to learn how to navigate cultures and taboos.

My first career was working as an international correspondent, covering a range of stories from Australian aboriginal land rights to interviewing Sinn Féin prisoners in Maghaberry prison. I then took to the stage, and upset the status quo by bringing to the mainstream my one-woman show, *Brown Girl in the Ring*. This upset *The Sunday Times*, by me claiming Queen Sophia Charlotte, the second Black Queen of England, grandmother of Queen Victoria (the first Black Queen of England, Philippa of Hainault, reigned in the 14th century). The show, which toured internationally, dramatized to my audiences that I was a throwback from the Royal Black Blood, claiming my right to the throne. To this day I am still called Queenie and asked, "Are you really related to the Royal Family?"

I have a Masters in Creative Writing, Education and the Arts from Sussex University, and was awarded an honorary doctorate of letters for my contribution to the African Diaspora from the University of East London. My first novel, *Borrowed Body*, republished as *The Banana Kid*, won the Mind Book of the Year award. I have written several plays and seven other books, including my first collection of poetry and plays, *Brown Girl in the Ring*. My cult play *Sin Dykes*, was a box-office sellout. My signature poem, "The Colour of My Skin," was exhibited in the National Portrait Gallery in London, has toured the UK, and is also part of a permanent installation, along with another of my poems, "Tangled Roots."

Two years after moving to Canada, I co-edited *The Great Black North: Contemporary African Canadian Poetry* with poet Kevan Cameron, which received two Alberta Book Awards in 2014: the Robert Kroetsch Award for Poetry and the Educational Award.

In 2016, I co-produced, along with Dr. Afua Cooper, ten poetic narratives telling the stories of Black Canadians from the 1700s to present day, which can be seen online at www.blackhalifax.com. I was the coach of the winning Edmonton team at the Canadian Festival of Spoken Word in 2011. In 2017, I won an award for my Services to Diversity at the European Diversity Awards celebrations, and was the winner of DIVA magazine's Literary Award for Poetry. In 2020, my work was published in *The Black Prairie Archives: An Anthology*, edited by Karina Vernon.

I now live in Canada where I am a co-founder of the Mindfulness Based Addiction Recovery (MBAR), an eight-week and four-week online program, and chair of the Vancouver Buddhist Centre. I am ordained into the Triratna Buddhist Order, and my Buddhist name is Vimalasara (she whose essence is stainless and pure). I have co-authored the award-winning self-transformation book, *Eight Step Recovery: Using the Buddha's Teachings to Overcome Addiction*, which is used in recovery meetings on several continents, and I am the author of *Detox Your Heart: Meditations for Healing Emotional Trauma*. I am one of the leading African Descent voices in the field of Mindfulness Approaches for Addictions, and I work as an inspirational speaker.

‖ And all of that is the bypassing story. It's what kept me alive. And to regain my sanity and my emotional health, I had to come face to face with the stories many of us push down for years, and carry around as toxic baggage every time we are activated.

My records say I was bleaching the colour of my skin before the age of four. The records also say I was so much of a problem I was put on drugs. I was moved from my third foster home at age four, because I was too much for my white foster mother. My new white carers in the orphanage named me Gruesome. I was sexually abused by their adopted son, and by some of the boys in my cottage.

I was always told, *Don't tell anybody* about the abuse, so when I first stole something from a teacher's purse, along with another boy, I told the whole class not to tell anybody. Only one person did.

At age eleven, I was placed back with my biological mother. She was given housing on the condition she take back her daughter. Needless to say, it didn't go so well. Although it almost cost me my sanity and my life, I did salvage a Black identity, but one that was black on the outside and white on the inside. My mother was taken to court, and I was placed back in an orphanage in London. At age thirteen, I began to hate the police; I was singled out by police for carrying a banner on an anti-Nazi march. I was mouthy: "Why are you picking on me, one of the only Black people on the march?" I was arrested, put in a cell, and a police woman searched me by ramming her hand up my crotch asking, "Are there any dangerous weapons up there?"

I lost a lot of childhood friends to accidental overdosing, suicide and murder. For the most part, I managed to live on the streets, but at fifteen I was incarcerated for shoplifting. I did eighteen months inside, much of that time in solitary confinement.

I came back out into the world, aged seventeen, with an eating disorder, addictive behaviours, and a juvenile record. This is also the story of some of my contemporaries. It's still the story of many young Black people today.

I have spent many a day being too scared to walk the streets from fear of being beaten up or killed by the police or by the National Front, a far-right fascist political party founded in the UK during the 1960s. The sus laws (from "suspected person"), stemming from 19th-century vagrancy legislation, were used predominantly against Black people as a discriminatory racial profiling tool. Today, many Black people walk the streets wary of these same threats.

While so many Black people are still suffering, I commit to using my success in life for the uplift of my people. I stand on the shoulders of my ancestors, and walk in the lineage of shamans, dedicating my life to helping people struggling in the hell realms of addictions and addictive compulsive behaviours—symptoms of multi-generational and epigenetic trauma. Until Black lives are valued and equal, I cannot rest from the struggle.

I am still your negro and *I am not your negro* is my truth.

Introduction

WHO IS THIS PERSON, named Valerie Jane Mason-John? Which part of this is my ancestral African name? I carry the DNA of slavery in many cells of my body: "civilized," labelled and packaged.

I Am Still Your Negro is a collection of social justice poetry exploring taboos and taboos within taboos. Witnessing Raoul Peck's documentary *I Am Not Your Negro*—a film inspired by James Baldwin's unfinished work, *Remember the House*—I felt the agony of my heart, and I thought, I'm still your negro, despite the fact that Baldwin was entrusting us with his profound wisdom a half-century ago.

This collection of poetic narratives, spoken word, and traditional poetic forms is also inspired by the literary movement Negritude, which came out of the Black Paris intellectual environment of the 1930s and 40s. Writers such as Aimé Césaire, Frantz Fanon, Léon Damas, and W. E. B. Dubois together asserted their Black identity through the French language. Ninety years later, there is still a need to react against the savagery of colonialism that still exists in both covert and overt forms, and against the superiority of the white domination in our countries of origin and in the African Diaspora.

The initial inspiration of all these poems is taken from the biographies and the collective experience of those of us who have been affected by the scattering of the African Diaspora, which, centuries later, continues to play out as the intergenerational trauma that my people experience. And then there is the voice of Yaata, a current which runs through this collection and which carries the spirit of Africa. Yaata's spirit inhabits centuries of wisdom, reminding us of our proud past.

Learning from these historical and spiritual circles of influence, I have told my own stories, rooted in the contemporary culture in which I grew and learned to survive. While I may be free from the mental slavery that Bob Marley sings about, my Black, Queer body is still incarcerated by the white, male, heteronormative gaze. I am a taboo within a taboo, and the impact on me and any of us in these categories has shaped people who have had to adapt to our painful realities. Our oppression has shaped our lives. In fact, I coined the term *FemGro* (a play on the word Negro) to define the intersectionality of my race and assigned gender at birth. Often my gender and race are inseparable. People either see Black woman, or glimpse my big dreadlocked stature and assume Black male. The Black female in the white gaze is often objectified, harassed, assaulted.

The Me Too movement is just scratching the surface of the viral epidemic of harassment and molestation of women's bodies. For Black Queer, Transgender, and Cisgender women, our skin colour and gender are under surveillance by the privileged who do not have to think about whether they will arrive home at night without having to dodge a bullet, deflect a knife, or escape misogynistic sexual assault or harassment. And some of the most horrific murders are against Black male-to-female transgender women.

And while I may not belong to a slave owner, and I may not belong to a man, the fact is Black women have grandfathers, fathers, husbands, sons, uncles, nephews, brothers and male cousins. The Black male body, perceived within the white gaze, has been profiled as brute, thug, and has become a weapon that is feared and needs to be shot dead. We have to live with the fact that our Black men are feared, and shot disproportionately at a higher rate than any other section of society. And Black transgender men are also at risk of this threat. When Black male and transgender male bodies are not being killed by the police, or murdered by white racist men, the prison cell and the mental health institutions have become the modern-day plantations where inmates are paid a minimum wage to produce goods that benefit giant industrial-military corporations as well as keeping the prisons functioning. Filmmaker Ava DuVernay in her documentary *13th* calls this the mass incarceration of Black people, which has become an extension of slavery.

The life expectancy of Black men has been curtailed by all these factors. A 2015 study by the *Guardian* investigated 1,134 deaths by law enforcement officers and concluded that young black men were nine times more likely than other Americans to be killed by police. It's almost become convenient for governments to turn away from the fact that the highest cause of death of Black men under the age of 30 is either being shot by the police or Black-on-Black homicides. Both are tragic symptoms of white supremacy and domination. Why aren't we doing something to deter this? It's no wonder that reparations and apologies have not been issued to us. Colonizers are still enslaving Black people.

And while we've witnessed Barack Obama, the first Black African American president, and while we've seen a Black African American woman, Meghan Markle, marry into the British royal family, we cannot sit back and think things have changed. The lives of Black men and women are still abysmal in many parts of the world. My people have had so much multi-generational loss.

We carry this loss as ancestral trauma. Many of us have become victims of drug and club culture, street crime, abandonment, mental health and child services systems, sexual abuse, eating disorders, and suicide, both directly and indirectly. It's no wonder that this intergenerational trauma has turned us against our own brothers, sisters and cousins. Because the colonizer has turned us against each other, we are killing each other, hating each other. Modern-day slavery has embittered us.

African descent communities in the Diaspora are more vulnerable to immigration laws, border controls, poverty, and many other inequities. Many countries in Africa still have some of the highest infant mortality rates in the world. Africa has been susceptible to climate change for years; flooding, mudslides, temperature rises and drought have caused many people to flee to other countries. Who is welcoming us with open arms?

People of Colour communities are some of the most vulnerable to climate change; if we value their lives, we would extend our valuing of the earth. If we are really going to do something about climate change, Black people, Indigenous people, and People of Colour must become an important concern of the Extinction Rebellion movement. It's urgent and we must act now. Yes, the planet is threatened. People are dying in Africa because of climate change, and Black people in the Diaspora are unfairly dying on the streets. When will Black lives matter?

These poems stretch across several continents and decades. I borrow from my oral tradition, and use stage poetry to bring alive narrative poems. I also experiment with various poetic forms—villanelles, sonnets and haiku—to explore sexual transgressions and violence. The poetic Narrator is the Supreme Being Yaata, from one of the Indigenous cultures of Sierra Leone. Yaata resides in the Land of Diamonds, Kono. It is believed that Yaata created humankind. The Supreme Being speaks through me to share the strength, resilience and pain of my ancestors. Yaata speaks in my voice to tell part of all our stories.

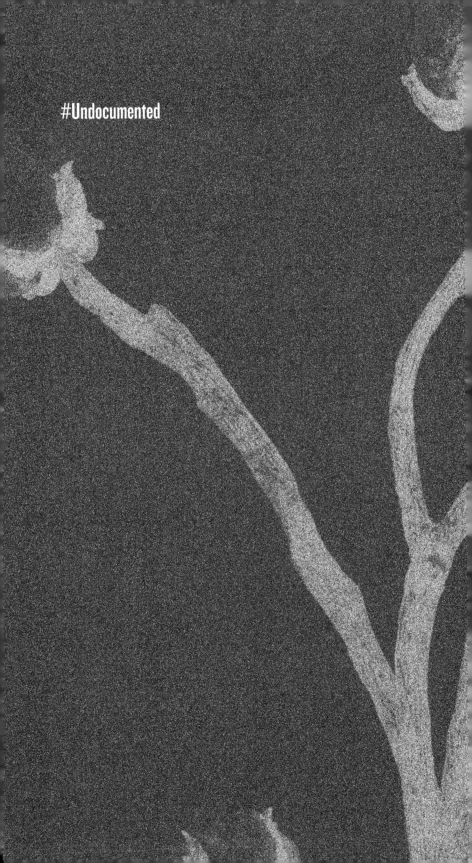

Back a Yard

Long ago, in the land of the Caribs and Arawaks, Sia's mother, while passing over to the other side, clutched her daughter's hand and said: "Promise me one ting. Mek sure yu dilute dis white blood we ave. Yu Gran Mudda suhvive de miggle passage, but she did lose har sanity, dignity and har apihtite fi talk. Har voice secreted from beneat har tongue jus afta I did bawn. She did get rape on de ship dat did transport har to Jamaica. She die de day afta I did give birt to yu. I too was rape, inna de cotton feel."

"Moomy, how come yu neva tell me dis before?" Sia cried.

"Stop yu nize. Listen to me good. Me nuh ave much longa and me need fi pass dis on. Yu nuh bawn a dis lan. Yu come from Africa. Is wah yu ere de white mon a call farrin, de dark continent. We white blood is a mistake. We haffi fix ih. Me ere seh some a di slaves weh escape in a di Jamaican hills, and dem revolt. Militant ones dem a call Maroons. Some even demand fi go back Africa de lan of we ancestors, where dem militants believe dem ave liberation. When it appen yu mek sure yu tek de ship wid dem. Yu ere me. It will tek yu to a place where yu will ave freedom."

"But Moomy a me home dis. Me blood fine, its yu blood."

"Me vex, me nuh finish, de Lawd has spare me a likkle more time. Promise me dis. Galong back a Africa. Let no slave owna rape yu. Yu ere me? And yu mus marry a full blood African. Me know seh a huge debt me know, but we blood line mus return back to Africa intact, a yu Gran Muddas lass wish." She grunted a little, her lungs gave up on life, and her eyelids closed.

"Moomy yu cyant die, not now, me need yu." Sia threw her body on top of her mother's.

Her mother woke, opened her eyes, and whispered in her daughter's ear: "Yaata, tek me back to Yaata." Her breath rasped and then she expired.

My Father's Prayer

My father who art in the universe

What on earth is your name

Will you ever come

Thy will be home

Dead or alive

Give me day or night your daily name

And I will forgive your sons

Forgiving all those who have colluded with your sins

And lead me not into more unhappiness

But deliver me from this pain

For thou have the power and the knowledge

Forever and ever

Of

All men.

Sticks and Stones

Sticks and stones did break my bones
And words did always hurt me.
My white mother told me never to moan.

She was old and cold as stone.
I was young and as scared as she.
Sticks and stones did break my bones.

I had no friends, so played alone.
I hated myself for being an adoptee.
My white mother told me never to moan.

A white child broke my jawbone.
He pulled me down onto my knees.
Sticks and stones did break my bones.

One day I was found crying on my own.
White children came over and pissed on me.
My white mother told me never to moan.

When there was blood on the kerbstone
My white mother tried to protect me.
Sticks and stones did break my bones
But she still told me never to moan.

During the 1960s and 70s in the UK, Black families were not considered suitable enough to adopt or foster a Black child.

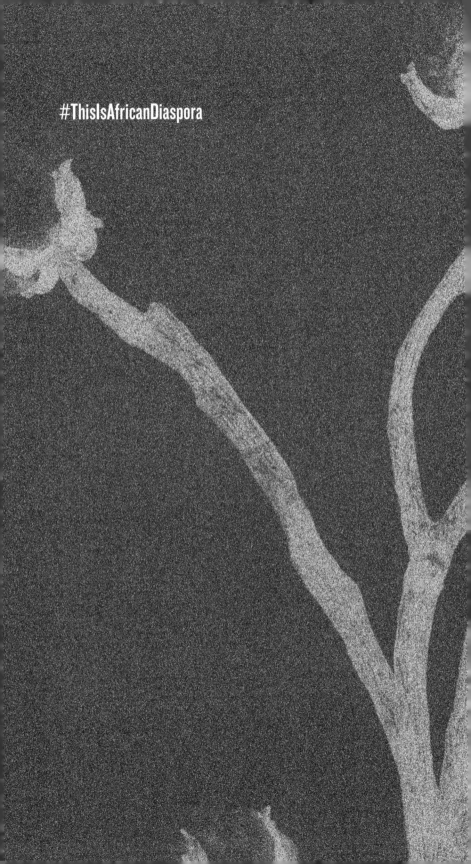
#ThisIsAfricanDiaspora

Yaata's Lament

I was born in the red-hot dust, among the luminous green foliage and the sweet-smelling fruits of the earth. My guardians left food at the base of my roots, and bowed down and worshipped the land they depended on. In return I protected them from the hot swelling sun with my luscious emerald green shade and sustained them with the abundant crops I produced all year round. And so my progeny were happy.

Then one day the Hungry Ghosts voyaged into my waters, arrived on my shores in their big tall ships. I told my progeny: "Befriend them. They are part of our human race." My people thought the men on the ships, with their pasty faces, were sick. They thought the men must have a bad fever with all the clothes they clustered upon their bodies under my blistering sun.

So my people gave them food and medicine in the hope they would recover. Some turned scarlet. But those who recovered burned a golden brown, and soon became strong.

I saw it coming, tried to warn my people not to tell them our secrets. My heavens opened and poured out my warning signs. Squalling rains and thunder came in February, months before the rainy season was due. My earth became mashed like fufu. But it was too late. The Hungry Ghosts knew all they needed to know. They climbed out of their tall leather boots and learned that barefoot was the way to tread.

In the middle of the night they stole up silently on my people with fishing nets, chains and guns. They herded them up like cattle, slaughtered them like pigs and beat the wretched survivors into a pulp. My guardians were destroyed, broken people. Those who survived—who were clamped at the feet, wrists and necks and dragged off to the ships—were never the same. Their spirits were crushed.

Their bodies sagged. They called out for me: "Yaata come nah. Punish we no more." They cried, threw libations at the trees, the mountains, the plants and everything that lived. Oh, how my progeny howled. My soil is stained with the blood of my people.

Then the Hungry Ghosts sailed back to my land, and with their hatchets, choppers and bulldozers they cleared my jungles. My trees were hacked down, severed and splintered. This ransom of my land is forever visible in the red dust that scratches the eyes.

The next time the Hungry Ghosts cursed my land with a visit they returned with their missionaries. They destroyed my idols, my artefacts, sacred stone deities, places of worship beneath the trees, beside the rivers and on top of the mountains. They pitched their wooden crosses at my holy sites and choked my people with their white Jesus, brainwashed them with their primitive laws, banished anything that did not conform to the union of Adam and Eve.

The backbone of my people broken to smithereens. Our religion, culture and language fractured almost beyond repair. Oh how I wept, the beliefs of my people corrupted by Christianity, with Islam charging fast behind.

But I, Yaata, still roamed the heavens, and many of my inhabitants continued furtively to worship my animals, trees, minerals and mountains. And I protected them the best I could, providing overgrowth to protect their places of prayer and treacherous tracks that only my people could find.

Not everything that is faced can be changed, but nothing can be changed until it is faced.

    —JAMES BALDWIN

The Ghost of Thomas Peters

Me slave name Thomas Peters
And me can read
Yes me can read
Real good good good

Me neva let me massa know me can read
Iza smart slave
Iza let me massa tink me need de newspapers
To keep me warm at night

1775 it was when de massa wife trow
She old papers at me feet
Me eyes catch de ad
Real good good good
Kings army needs recruits
And me eyes clap down pon de words
Negroes we need you too

Lawd ave Mercee pon me
Him a give me dese two good eyes
For a reason
Him a give me dese two strong legs
For a reason
Him a give me dis newspaper
For a reason

Me run and me run and me run to de flour mill

And me whisper to me Fren

Look, Dunmore Proclamation

Come na follow we

We gonna be free

Come join de Kings army

And dem look pon me as if me craze

Wat wrung wid you

Why you so uppity

We eat good, we dress good

And we get few lashes

We stayin

Runaway slaves get catch

Runaway slaves loose dem feet

Runaway slaves get kill

But me na care

Me just run and me run and me run

Just as me did in 1760

26 years old

Runnin wid me Egba clan

When de net came tunderin down

Pon dis Yoruba village

Dem a shackle we neck to neck

Chain we wrist to wrist

Clamp we foot to foot

Frog-marched to Bunce Island

De slave castle in Sierra Leone

Sold for a bottle of rum

And a pouch of tobacco

And shipped we to de Americas
Wid me aunties, uncles, cousins, sisters, brothers
All of dem met dere demise
Tossed overboard

Watched me fadda sell
Me mudda sell
And listen to she scream
As dem transport me down south
To French Louisiana
Where Iza try fi escape tree times
Until dem sell me to de Campbell plantation
De first time me run
Dem place an iron belt pon me waist
And dem brand me wid a hot iron rod

But me na care me still run
And Iza been runnin and runnin for me Freedom
Until de Kings army accept we
Yes believe
De Kings army accept we
Yes believe
De Kings army accept plenty Black people
Believe

And we fight longside dese white people
And we help to maintain de crown
And we help to preserve de crown

Iza fight for me Freedom
Iza loyal for me Freedom
Iza defend for me Freedom

Dem promise we a guinea, land and me Freedom
But when de revolutionary war was over
Dem try to put me back pon de block
Dem try to auction me off
Gawaan Peters dey say show massa yo strong ape arm
Good for work on rice plantations
Gawaan Peters dey say walk roun
So de massa can see how spry yo is

But me neva going back pon de block
Iza proud Black Loyalist
Iza proud Black Sergeant
Iza proud Black Revolutionary
Iza named the first Black American Hero

Some of we didn't mek it
Dem a kidnap we
And sell we back into slavery

And some of we did mek it
Dem a give we our paper
And we set sail for Nova Scotia in 1783

And when we arrive
We look for we land
And dem point to some swamp
Me say where we land
And dem say here yo swamp
And me larf and me larf until me belly full

Coz me get me swamp and me get me Freedom
Coz me get me swamp and me start a Revolution
Coz me get me swamp and me collect plenty signed petitions
Coz me get me swamp and me get to visit Inglan

Iza stand in front of de Royal Government

Iza rightfully complain

Coz de land mash up

And it hav no grain

Coz we fight for we Freedom

And dem want to put we back into serfdom

But me mek good fren wid a white abolitionist name Clarkson

He promise we passage back to de homeland

Im offer to help recruit negroes to repatriate

And when we return we get fi recruit me people

From Annapolis Valley, Birchtown, Halifax, Shelburne

Wid a Cato Perkins, Moses Wilkinson, William Ash

Yes believe we some of de foundin Black fathers

Of a Free Town in Sierra Leone

We lef right here

From de Halifax port

Men, women, pickne

1,100 of we volunteer to return to de homeland

Wid me as dere Speaker General

Clarkson as dere Governor General

When we set foot pon de land in 1792

Me people, yes, me people

Choose white Clarkson

As dere proper General

And me heart brek

Yes me heart brek

Four months later
Mosquitos suck me blood
And me expire from malaria
Leavin me wife seven pickne
To carry me name back
To de Egba clan
Where Iza always be a strong proud
Yoruba man

I Am Africa

I am Africa

Polished by the Saharan sun
Blue-black, red-black, brown-black
Blonde hair, blue-eyed, thick-lipped
Swinging in my hips
Swimming in my genes
Ebonized like my Madagascar trees

I am Africa

A galaxy of 54 countries
9 territories
2 disputed states
Orating dialects of over
3,000 overtures
I am language literate
Language articulate
Laughing, drumming, dancing
A cappella voices telling my story

I am Africa

Diamonds, bauxite, iron
Shaken and taken
From my red-hot earth
Blasted from my mountains

Sold by the corporates
Ransack, pillage, death
Blood leeched from my peoples

I am Africa

Pharaohs, gods, idols, kings, queens
Pyramids, temples
Dictators, child soldiers, rebels
Muslims, Christians, traditional
Amputation, starvation, ethnic cleansing
I am seeking reparations

I am Africa

Pillaged from my villages
Chipped from my ancestral line
Chained to my sisters and brothers
Cattled and sardined
As we journeyed the Middle Passage
Dead and alive
Refashioned to fit into the colonizers' narcissistic mould

I am Africa

Desert, jungle, forest
Mountain, ocean
Urbanized, gentrified, petrified forest
A kingdom of nature
A safari of animals
Missing their ivory, horns, skins

I am Africa

The mother of all peoples
The mother of all nations
Birthing the first humanoid
Civilizing the first society
Robbed of my riches
Compensated with poverty, famine, AIDS, infant mortality, war

I am Africa

What is there left to take?
Africa?
You can never take Africa
Because Africa is the spirit that will always roam my continent

I am Africa

Inspired by Ahmed "Knowmadic" Ali

African Feet

Stripped raw
Peeling back ancient memories

African feet stand firm
A thousand years ago
Belonging to the proud Sapi tribe
Who carved their steps
Along the banks of the west coast

African feet shackled
Five hundred years ago
Pillaged from their homeland
Forced to toil in cotton fields
Whipped sore
Sap oozing rivers
Of sweat, blood and tears

Beating the rhythms
Of their lost drums
Un-united in the States of America

Today, African feet are Muslim feet
Muslim feet are African feet
Running from Islamophobia
In the Great White North of Canada

Terror flailing in our hearts
African feet displaced in the angry streets
Athletes' feet
Dancing feet
Convicted feet
Protesting feet
In this Un-united Kingdom

Peeled to the core
The soles of African feet
Uprising along this scattered journey

The Windrush

Departing from Kingston, Jamaica, the British ship Empire Windrush
brought one of the first large groups of postwar Caribbean immigrants to
London in 1948.

Dem did sey she pregnance
Cum a sea full a mi
Weighing har down eena har shoe dem
Dresses, coco, mangoes an baggy an arl

Dem did sey de ship nearly sink
Mi mumma nebah sleep a wink
Dem did sey Inglan full a promise
But arl mi mumma do a reminisce

She did stow away
An hide betwix de trunk dem
She cum doh
Coz mi puppa cum too

She stuff full a mi
An mi a gunna mek har rich
Har belly bulge stretch
Sea sick
Marnin sick
Home sick

She did hear sey London street
Pave wid gold
But a wah kina Nancy story dis?
Obeah a play him tricks
Mi mumma an mi puppa a feel him licks

Mi mumma cry ebbry night
An scribbled bak home to har granny
London street dem pave wid sleet
An har granny scribble bak
Mi did tink yuh sail pon de Goldrush
No Granny, de Windrush
An de street pave wid sleet

Sleet? A wah dat?
Some kina fancy name fi yuh man
Granny skrawl bak

Mi bawn pon de dot
Is wah appen to black peoples time?
Mi mumma arsk de nurse
Mi puppa sneer
Inglan is a bitch

Mek mi tell yuh Inglans crime
Nuh rice an peas
Nuh stew pot or dumplin
Nuh ackee an salt fish
Nuh cassava leaf

Mi mumma an mi puppa survive doh
Malnutrition
Humiliation
Interrogation
Assimilation

Welcome to de lan a honey an milk
De poster dem did sey bak a yard
Sweet honey an money
Obeah a play him tricks
A giv mi mumma an puppa pure licks

But mi gunna be arl right doh
Coz mi mumma pray fi har likkle pickne
Ebbry night, an mi grow jus fine
While mi granny curse
Coz de ongley gold she see when she cum a
Farrin Inglan
Is de gold eena mi puppa teet
An de cuppa tea Lawd a wah dat?
Weh de bush tea? Ganja tea?

Mi mumma she sing to mi ebbry night doh
She coo eena mi two ear dem
Arl har pickne a go be arl right
Despite de night
She set sail pon
De Windrush

I Am Still Your Negro

I was your Negro
Captured and sold
I am still your negro
Arrested and killed

You made me a slave
You made me homeless
You made me an immigrant
You made me illegal

I was your Negro
Captured and sold
I am still your negro
Arrested and killed

You made me a shooter
You made me a mugger
You made me a hustler
You made me a pimp

I was your Negro
Captured and sold
I am still your negro
Arrested and killed

You made me a single baby mother
You made me a crack baby
You made me fatherless
You made me a drop-out

I was your Negro
Captured and sold
I am still your negro
Arrested and killed

You made me an entertainer
You made me an athlete
You made me a writer
You made me a caretaker

I was your Negro
Captured and sold
I am still your negro
Arrested and killed

You made me paranoid
You made me weapon
You made me predator
You made me intimidator

I was your Negro
Captured and sold
I am still your negro
Arrested and killed

You made America Great Again
You made America White Again
You made me a Nigger Again
You made me Hate Again

I was your Negro
Captured and sold
I am still your negro
Arrested and killed

Another One Bites the Dust

Strobed red and blue, crazed and flooded by police light
She cradles her 18-year-old son stiffening on her breasts

Murdered by cops in a gunfight
Resisting wrongful arrest

She wails, *My son is dead*
Not even old enough to graduate

Smothered, covered in his bloodshed
Killed by fear and senseless hate

Collapses and uncontrollably blubbers
Cradling, soothing, screaming, lifeless

Who cares? Just another black body dead in the gutter
One more death, corrupt and senseless

Another one bites the dust

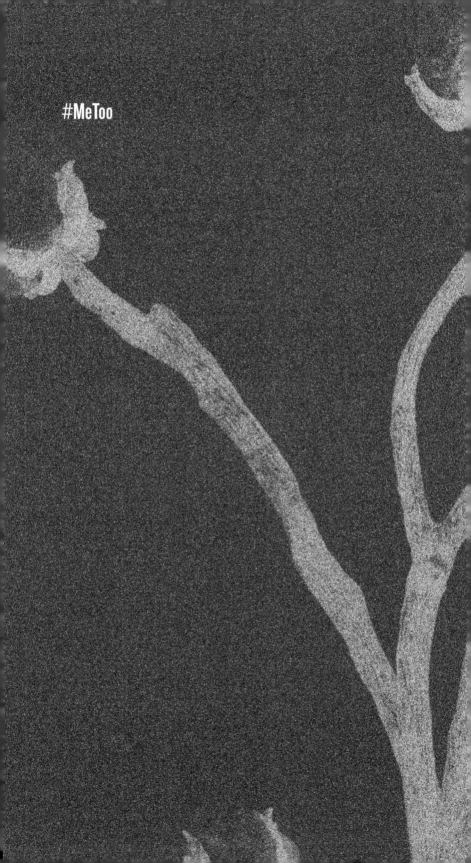
#MeToo

Yaata's Yowl

One day some of the Hungry Ghosts became bold, followed my faithful custodians, and they discovered one of the many secrets of my land. They found some of my precious minerals—rutile, bauxite, gold, iron ore. Not content, they blasted my land apart to see what else lay deep beneath my earth. My spirits were disturbed. Finally they found part of my life source: Diamonds. My land could not survive this catastrophic rape. The sirens shrilled, my animals took flight, and then the earth collapsed. Rocks, dust and my crumbling earth sunk twenty feet lower.

Climate changed forever. The greed for minerals that keep the environment regulated culminated in mudslides, earthquakes, droughts, floods, starvation, and the threatened extinction of my precious animals, destabilizing my peaceful society. War ravaged my land, and spilled blood onto the hot dusty earth. Sand-Sand boys juggled their pans for rough diamonds, while the big fat pasty men in their jeeps ogled their reflections in my gems. Many of them descendants of the men who lynched my people and spoiled my women. Ripped their children from their breasts, and sold them for rum.

Who did the Hungry Ghosts think they were, discarding my children? Have they no remorse? How dare they turn their backs on my children just because they feared they would be too dark for the European eye. Have they no respect? Giving birth is not like the children's game Pass the Parcel. It is their duty to raise these children with all the love in the world. My offspring are not responsible for the Hungry Ghosts' lust. Were these men stupid enough to think that their offspring would never haunt them in their waking dreams, sleepless nights and cold sweats? Yaata, the Supreme Being, always knows that this gift of mingled blood is not for you to reject. You may think you can shut Yaata out, deny my existence. Never. You will never have a peaceful night's sleep.

Africa is the host of one of the largest mineral industries in the world and still my people are poor. You pillaged my land, raped my women, and shackled my men. Their spirits will rise again, and you will hang your heads in disgrace.

It is certain, in any case, that ignorance allied with power is the most ferocious enemy justice can have.
—JAMES BALDWIN

Business

Hard — Stiff — Wet
As it rams its way
Through forbidden thighs.

Pulsating on her door.

A strangled breath
Absent without leave
Ejects this useless key.

Poised once more for action.

Head on head
A pungent rod
Throbbing between two lips.

Hijacked out of her body.

She stands erect
Ready for business
Topless and hand relief is all he gets.

He's left gagging for sex.

She smiles
Takes control
Her burglar alarm has gone off.

Golden Virginia

Golden Virginia from his tin
Stale yellow stains on his fingers
Caressing her forbidden breasts
Beneath his library
Of shelves crammed with stories
About little girls
In search of their Grandmas

His big hairy rough hands scour
Her unblemished skin
His long tongue probes
Caustic against her coconut drops
Golden Virginia
Still moist in his tin
Ready to be fingered, skinned
Roll-ups to smoke
Rollies bumsucked between his lips

The Villain

Mummy what is a penis?
It's what men have, Alice.

I played with angels and changed my name.
In bed at night he came. And I felt shame.

Why does it have two golf balls?
So their eggs are warm and comfortable.

I confessed to God our special game.
He told me to pray until daylight.
I played with angels and changed my name.

Why do men have eggs?
To make beautiful babies like you and Meg.

He told me I was to blame.
Made me promise never to fight.
He came. And I felt shame.

How do the eggs make Meg and me?
By Daddy placing his penis inside me.

He lifted my covers and made me tame.
My body lost all its appetite.
I played with angels and changed my name.

Where do the eggs grow Mummy?
Inside my womb, which lives in my tummy.

I hated him and all his games.
Again he came. He stayed all night.
He came. And I felt shame.

Can Meg and I grow babies?
Yes of course, when you become ladies.

When I grew round, he wasn't the same.
Instead, he visited Meg out of sight.
Meg played with angels. I changed her name.
He came. And I felt shame.

Mummy I think Daddy's eggs are in my stomach.
It's time for bed now. I'll play you some Bach.

The Perfect Road

On this road lives number 1
Perfect people — Perfect house

On this road lives number 3
Stands erect — A semi-detached

On this road lives number 5
Trimmed hedges — Rose gardens

On this road lives number 7
Stained-glass windows — Candelabra

On this road lives number 9
Land Rover — Red Aston Martin Coupe

On this road lives number 11
Police Inspector — Midwife

On this road lives number 15
White people — Black nannies

On this road lives number 17
Bridge parties — Caviar, cucumber sandwiches

On this road lives number 19
Cuban cigar stubs — Prozac

On this road lives number 21
Chihuahua puppies — Private schools

On this road lives number 23
Action Man — Princess Barbie

On this road lives number 25
Call of Duty — Children screaming

On this road lives number 27
Pulled curtains — Moonlight Sonata

On this road lives number 29
Plastic smiles — Dark glasses

The Couplet

This is the day I became his mate
He took me to a village fete.

I held his hand   Felt very proud
We danced to music   Exciting, loud.

Sampled brandies   Played tombola
Sat on the grass   He rolled me over.

I said, *No, not here on the front lawn*
He took my hand   Led me to a barn.

He pulled me tight   Gave me a kiss
I pulled away   Tried to resist.

He unzipped my dress   I pushed him away
He pulled down his pants   What could I say?

He jumped on top   Pinned me down
I gave in   He knocked me around

He stood   Shadowed me lying on the floor
Accused me loud   *Prude! Black Whore!*

He cleaned me up   Promised it would be all right
I knew he was lying   I cried all night.

I rang my white friends   Told them my fury
They listened   Accused me, Judge and Jury

They sentenced me   I was to blame
Since that day   I've slouched with shame.

#MeToo

Me and You

Who?
Almost everyone has a story to brew
Not just the Hollywood crew
It's everywhere you look
In every cranny and nook
This sordid tyranny
This criminal irony
Some men harassers
Some women perpetrators
Some men embarrassed
Some women harassed
Culture grows the predators
Culture harvests the predators
Women and girls packaged for the taking
Women and girls silent and aching
Sexualized, commodified
Few of us speaking out

Heaven was a girl who
Lived a life of hell before she cursed
Mother's boyfriend touching
Mother is ignoring
But Heaven found courage
Even though she was discouraged
She spoke out and told Tarana Burke

Who dared not say to Heaven
Me Too

It took Tarana nine years
To realize women's and girls' suffering
Was numbing and buffering
So out of control
Our stories flushed down a sinkhole
Nine years to pay homage
To Heaven's courage
Founding the Me Too movement
Giving girls and women of colour equity
On Myspace for empowerment and empathy

2017 Weinstein suffers his downfall
When a streetwise white woman Alyssa Milano adds to
a borrowed quote from a friend: *If you've been sexually harassed or*
assaulted write "me too" as a reply to this tweet
It exploded, metastasized, was tweeted
More than half a million times
Hashed by 4.7 million people in 12 million posts
During the first 24 hours of its new unveiling

And one of the world's most powerful men
Accused of sexual misconduct by more than a dozen women:
Leeds, Anderson, Harth, Heller, McDowell, Virginia, Sullivan,
Dixon, McGillivray, Crooks, Stoynoff, Murphy, Drake, Laaksonen,
Zervos, Searles, Carroll

But he's still President of the USA, right?
Fake Fact?
No!
Fake News?
No!

He cries: *I am a victim of one of the great political smear campaigns*
in the history of our country
But despite his Non-Disclosure
His crimes get exposure
Cohen pawns off 130,000 dollars that could not silence the Storm
Even though he boasts, *When you're a star,*
They let you do...anything
To all the women who've made his prey-list
He gives his vitriolic hiss
She's not my type
And guess what? He must be innocent
The American public voted for him

And who believes you or me?

And if the Glitterati can get away with it
So can our families, friends, colleagues
It's not coincidental that it's become political
Politicians, Royals, Socialites, Entertainers, Film Stars, Athletes,
Medical Professionals, Priests, Monks, Nuns, Parents, Teachers,
Siblings, Cousins, Neighbours, Babysitters, Friends,
People we Trust

America's Supreme Court Judge
Kavanaugh is not going to budge
Ford's word's devalued
Kavanaugh's lies valued

Professor Anita Hill called out Clarence Thomas
Accused of flat-out perjury
Told she was a little bit nutty
And a little bit slutty
Are you a scorned woman?

Everyone we trusted
Which is why they're not busted
Coz it's ok to be lusted
Quid pro quo
Crimes in plain sight
In full light
No need for cover
Presidents have immunity
Groping with impunity
Family and friends have immunity
Often inviting predators into their homes
To prey on their daughters
Welcome! You're gold!

And while women reel with disdain
Complicit silence emerges again
Women shunned into cover-up
Afraid of losing their jobs
Afraid of not being believed
Afraid of being demoted
Afraid of retaliation
Afraid of being stalked
Afraid of being smeared

Children, Teens are touched up
Because nobody listens
Because they must be lying
Because they must be imagining
Because they must be dreaming
Because they don't like the new boyfriend
Because they were precocious
Because they're not taken seriously

Hashtag #MeTeen
And now she's called a Has-Been
Humiliated and labelled unclean
Her fault for being obscene
Justice just a smoke screen
No one accused
Most are excused
Girls are left bruised
Sad, subdued and confused

It's all just after all
Harmless fun
Boys being boys
Using girls as toys
What's up with all the noise?
It's what men do — Normal
Hormonal
Business as usual
Endure it!

In the office, in the dressing room, in the washroom, in the
corridor, during rush hour, on the bus, on the train, in taxis, in
the lineup, on the streets, in the bedroom, in the ensuite, on the
stairwell, in the kitchen, in the dining room, in the garden shed,
behind closed doors, in the family car

Suggesting, looking, insinuating, winking, upskirting, sexting,
humiliating, promising, threatening, feeling, fingering,
touching, penetrating, masturbating

And while they're tossing
They are hoping we'll applaud
But there's no titillation
Just thoughts of castration
With messages trending on your screen
Snapchatted
Instagrammed
Pinterested
Twittered
#MeToo — They've done it again

We're told, *Too fat, Too ugly*
You deserve it, You asked for it
We're told, *Keep it backstage*
Angry women and girls on the rampage
Volcanic anger, erupting rage
We're told, *Brush it under the carpet*
Nobody gives a shit

Keep silent
People may become violent
Shut the fuck up
The family may break up
The world's biggest hush-up
We grit our teeth, even smile

Pretend we like it for a while
Then we get the balls
And Tell All
Just like Heaven
Fessing up a cartload of dung

The mudslinging begins
And we go on trial
While the prosecutors demand
How tight were your clothes?
How short was your skirt?
How low was your top?
Were you drunk?
Were you wearing a bra?
Were you egging him on?
Did you make advances?
Did you agree to a drink?
Did you give a come on?
Did you enjoy it?
Well what did you fucking expect?

Good Guys don't take advantage of women and girls
Good Guys don't say *More More More*
Good Guys don't say *How do you like it, how do you like it*
Good Guys don't get the cameras rolling or the action going
Good Guys will grab you off the dance floor
Put your clobber back on
And Uber you home before you're hit upon

Bad Guys seem to think
No means Yes
Yes means No
Excuse me
Good Guys know that No means No
Yes means Yes and Yes may become a No
No is not a hard-on
Or playing hard to get
Just to make a dude wet
No means No
Got a problem
Read my lips S T O P

What if we said No, and said No a thousand times until we are heard
What if you looked your predator in the eye and said No
Assertively
Without flinching
Without worrying if he calls you a Bitch
Or throws a fit
What if you told someone
And the world around you fell apart
What if we all said
#METOO
#METEEN
#NOMORE #YOUREBUSTED

Playing Dead

Curled up in my mother's bed
Tight like a screw. Back to back
I can't sleep. I'm playing dead.
I simulate sleep. Avoid her smacks.
Daydream off to somewhere snug.
Soft warm fingers trace my spine.

I roll over. Hoping for a hug.
It's hard playing dead. I feel divine.
Fingers stroke my new-formed breasts.
She spreads my legs. I wet the bed.
I am aroused, unable to rest.
But I'm still playing dead.

She abandons me for a Marlboro Light.
I'm left aching for tomorrow night.

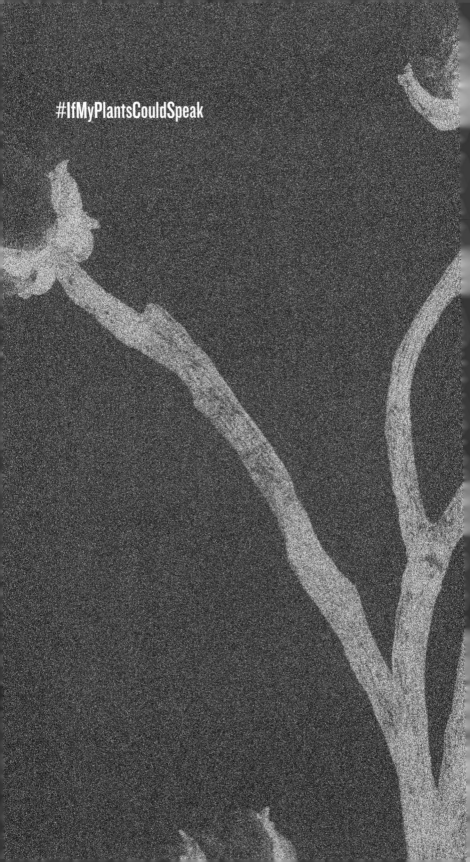
#IfMyPlantsCouldSpeak

Yaata's Groan

Yaata never dies. Yaata pervades all nature. I belong deep down, in my red-hot earth. My animals, trees, plants and minerals are the breath of life. My animals, plants and minerals all belong to the Supreme Being. They have been enslaved, domesticated and manifested in many ornamental forms and guises.

Look around and you will see me in shop windows, in garden centres, furniture shops and adorning almost every human being in some shape or form. I have been indentured into domestic service in the West, living in plant pots, mounted in jewelry and worn on the human body. You stuff and mount my animals in your lounges, you lay my precious animals' skins as rugs on your floors and you still smuggle home ivory, skulls and skeletons. Beware: you never know who you have taken home with you.

What blasphemy. My Supreme Being exploited as gifts of human love, trophies of human greed and decoration for human homes. My sacrosanct rites abused and degenerated. My plants have learned to stand calm in your households and observe every flaw. Stories are steeped into their spines. Their branches carry the knowledge, just as if they were at home in Africa, tending to my people. Every cell holds a different memory, an altered interpretation of the family history into which they have been adopted. And while you admire my dead animals, their spirits haunt your homes.

My animals, plants and minerals have never been enough. You stole my people and destroyed their sacred family constellation. It has been ravished by miscegenation, incarceration, violation and institutionalization. The bearers of my children were never meant to raise them alone. They were never meant to be robbed of their menfolk. My women and their children were never meant to be flawed by greed, hatred and delusion.

Dis-eased by fake civilization and homogenization, my women and their children have become slaves of the Western mirage. My children are slaves in your prison system. Until you face your demons and embrace the children of Mother Africa, the past will not be swept away by my winds. The past is in this present moment.

Did the Hungry Ghosts not realize there would be a price to pay? Their lust for my women has made some of their children as black and brown as my people. The Devil they feared in us is now lurking in their families. Can they not see the Devil is their delusion? My people are sacrosanct to this land, and were not born to feed the white man's domination. Neither were they born to serve. Black, brown, red, yellow, we will continue to populate.

This is the yowl of Yaata, who still resides in the people, trees, plants and animals that survived the brutality. Stop killing my children. Stop imprisoning my children. Stop raping my children. Stop stealing my children. They have become your children, and when you see that Black lives matter, all lives will matter, and you will begin to think well of my offspring and value all life, no matter what race, colour or creed.

To accept one's past—one's history—is not the same thing as drowning in it; it is learning how to use it.
—JAMES BALDWIN

Yellowknife

This poem is based on the first lesbian sexual assault case to be tried in Canada. In 1955 a white woman, "Laura" (a pseudonym), took Willimae Moore, an African American woman, to court for gross indecency in Yellowknife, Northwest Territories. Ms. Moore was found guilty. She and her white Canadian companion, Beatrice Gonzales, left town shortly after the prosecution. Even though Moore subsequently appealed the decision and won, her name was tarnished forever.

When it was a mere 20 below, I'd think,
Boy this is a great day, I can push back
my parka hood. I was used to New York winters,
this was nothing. 1953, Yellowknife,
in love with Beatrice Gonzales.
Followed her home to her native Canada.

Found work in a government office typing pool.
Some of us slept on the floor
when it was too cold to go home.
We'd fall asleep exchanging stories of our past.
Some women made it clear to me
my type of life was quite foreign.
They had absolutely no interest in me.

I made it clear I was not desperate.
That would be foolish.
Beatrice was a professional woman
of good standing, Vice Principal.
I was content with my comfortable life.

Now, you see, had I been a man, I could have got away
with touching a woman's cleavage, lifting
her petticoat up, even rubbing against her genitals.
If the woman tried to press charges,
she would be told she had encouraged it.
Asked what was she doing alone in a room,
with a man who wasn't her husband?
Told she must have made advances.

An attempted kiss would have been considered
trifling. Nothing to write home about.
Headline read: *First Same-Sex "Lesbian" Sexual Assault Prosecution.*
Branded a freak of nature.

The public needs to be protected.
Yellow Knives were out to get me.
Gross indecency was my crime.
Nobody asked me any questions.
Guilty on a white woman's evidence alone.

In court Laura claimed that she looked up at me
from her desk. I was supposed
to have looked strangely at her,
a rather concentrated look.
She claimed to look down. She said
I grabbed hold of her, tried to kiss her.
As she pushed me away,
I was to have said, *You're very cruel,*
and she began to cry.

Of course I looked at her.
Even undressed her with my eyes.
And she undressed me too.
Exotic, she whispered.
In the next breath spat out, *You beast*.
She locked eyes with me,
our lips brushed and she cried,
No, stop! I can't. I'm not strange like you.

I was the first woman arrested and tried
in a Canadian court: gross indecency
against another woman.
I was Yellowknifed
I was Black.
Guilt?

The Binge

Leftovers from brunch
Food for an army of pigs
The trash man appears

Full speed down a hill
A binge in the driver's seat
Can't stop got to eat

Stuffing to the brim
Full! A nine months' pregnancy
Her waters erupt

Dial 9-1-1
A frenzied bulimic purge
Emptied. Inside out

The VindaLoo

Hinged to the fridge door
Dislocated at the jaw
As she salivates
Over a curried heaven

Strobe lights judder before her glazed eyes
As she munches her way through paradise

Cream cakes smudged all over her face
Italian spaghetti whipping her chest
Rice hail-stoning onto her lap
Chicken bones splayed all over her toes

A compost bin spilling around her feet
Her binge not yet complete
Not enough, compelled to eat

Ice cream freezes her in slow motion
As frozen foods slalom down her throat
Thawed by skidding litres of Diet Coke
What a joke
She belches on its giddy gas
Stuffing more down, on her arse

Then purge, girl, head first
Before you faint, before you burst
Puke up the foulest stew
Into yesterday's VindaLoo

Anorectic

The Doctor says, *You will die if you don't eat.*
Mum and Dad are unsympathetic.
All I dream of is eating sweets.

I allow one carrot as a treat.
I spend all day teaching athletics.
The Doctor says, *You will die if you don't eat.*

I begin to binge on sweetmeats.
I down plenty of diuretics.
All I dream of is eating sweets.

I swallow vitamins, a way to cheat.
My friends say I'm becoming neurotic.
The Doctor says, *You will die if you don't eat.*

I refuse to eat, no mean feat.
I am diagnosed: Extreme Anorectic.
All I dream of is eating sweets.

My parents bribe me with a break to Crete.
I have tantrums and become frenetic.
The Doctor says, *You will die if you don't eat.*
All I dream of is eating sweets.

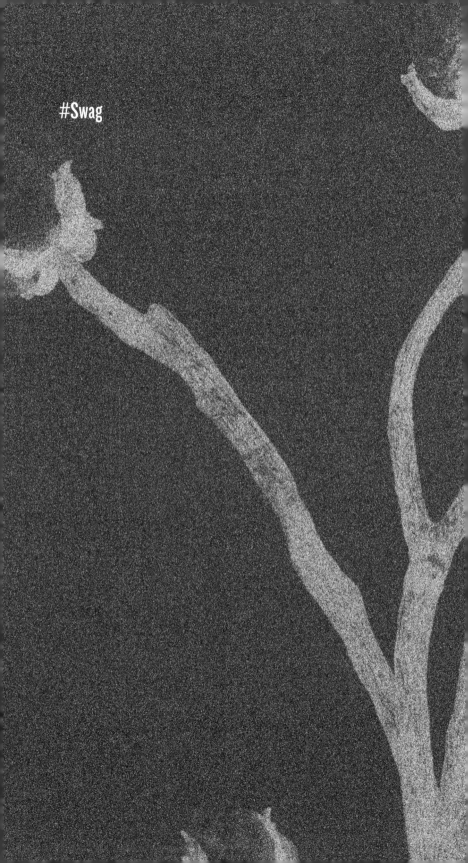

Yaata's Manifesto

Bredren, Sistren, is you so foolish to think you can outwit Yaata?
Did I not teach you anything during your initiation ceremony?
Did you offer up your brains as a sacrifice when the elders
taught you to dance on your feet and spin on your head when
conducting sanctified rituals?

Did you lose your balls when we buried you underground to see
if you had the courage to stay alive? Did you not have any respect
for your ancestors?

You imbeciles! Your brains are designed to guide you skillfully
through life and not to exploit them by conjuring up amazing
plots to protect you from your lies. Have you forgotten everything?
How my diamonds are the source of all life that grows from my
soil, the tools for shamans to do their healing work and minerals
to protect you from evil spirits. You have sold my blood.

Do you think you are knowledgeable enough to deceive me? My
minerals will haunt you. Your weapons will annihilate you. The
money you received from minerals and drugs will last not much
more than a decade. Designer brands have become your Gods,
and Rappers your Supreme Beings. Your big houses, big cars,
designer clothes will become worthless. You are indeed some of
my progeny who are still victims and caught in the vicious cycle
of slavery.

My sacred diamonds held earth's crater together, while my jungles, forests, bush, rainforest absorbed unwanted carbon in the atmosphere. When the Hungry Ghosts began blasting my land for diamonds, radioactive pollutants seeped into my drinking waters, the Harmattan winds in the dry seasons spread contaminated dust from the mines and some of you were never the same. No longer did you worship these precious stones as your spirit guides. Instead you began killing each other over the diamonds in the ground.

And today you are killing each other over postcodes. I pray your children do not make the same mistakes so that my cries perish on your funeral pyres.

Yes, you have lost your ancestral lands, your languages, cultures and names. Yes, you have been defined by the white gaze, confined by white laws, and your skin and your religion have become weapons for destruction. Beware, you too could end up dead one day and stuffed like my animals in a front room or hidden in a museum vault.

Turn to your modern philosophers for wisdom. Bob Marley urges you to "Emancipate yourselves from mental slavery. None but ourselves can free our minds."

Every time you pull the trigger or stab and exhilaration fuels your body, know that while you are dead to all the ways that society has condemned you, denied you and invalidated you, you are not empowered when you kill another.

As Malcolm X warned: "If you're not careful, the newspapers will have you hating the people who are being oppressed, and loving the people who are doing the oppressing."

While some of you are moved to forgive and love the people who have been oppressing you, you are now killing your brothers and sisters, and mothers and fathers.

Alice Walker says: "The most common way people give up their power is by thinking they don't have any."

This rage that many of you so understandably walk around with can be the energy to transform your life. You "Get up, stand up, stand up for your rights" by loving yourself, your whole being, and knowing your life is worth more than just 18 years on this earth. Your life is worth more than living a life of crime. Your life is the life of every one of us. You are not alone. I see the goodness in every one of you. Water the seeds of love inside you; they are there waiting for you to love your wounded selves.

To be a Negro in this country and to be relatively conscious is to be in a rage almost all the time.

—JAMES BALDWIN

The Front Line

Face to face. Suited and booted.
Porsches nose to nose. Gangstas cut eye, suck teeth.
Dressed to kill, streets looted.
People dread they're out to thieve.

Mugshots Black, decorated with scars.
Caught on camera robbing the streets, tooled up to kill.
National media superstars
Both on the run, hiding out from the Old Bill.

Fallen out as a posse, they argue and fight.
Charlie and Brown have made them both bitter.
Hands on guns in the middle of the night.
Both wounded as they fall into the gutter.

Cell phones flash, as they make a pact to dial 9-9-9.
Both dead next time they meet on the front line.

Old Bill *is British slang for police ;* Charlie *is cocaine;* Brown *is heroin.*

Sixty Seconds

Sweat beading on her brow
Hands clammy
Fingers taut but nimble
Primed to make their catch

Gentlemen's pockets on their bums and breasts
Ladies' handbags on their wrists and waists

60 seconds
60 dollars
60 pounds

She bumps and jostles her crowd
Slides away
Disappears
With the weight of their salary

Stalk Time

You must be adept
For cell phone theft

It's snatch and grab
In the main drag

They spot the latest Android
The rush enjoyed

As they snatch your phone
And run back home

But please rest assured
You will be insured

Your provider will send another
To replace the stolen other

And if it's not
You can buy cheap stock

In your local pub
But check it's not a dud

So they feel well sweet
With your Android treat

They dash your SIM card
Coz by now it's a discard

They've got pay as you talk
So they pose as they walk

They ring a mate on their new Samsung
And invite them out to hang

But he's on a contract
Which is a sad fact

As he can't pay bills
Then he can't sell pills

His line's gone dead
Before nuff said

So they press redial
And wait for a while

But they can't get through
So their plans go askew

So they join a local gang
And learn their text slang

They start trading Motorola
For ounces of marijuana

Exchanging WAP Alcatel
For hard drugs and collateral

So if you have a new iPhone
That you treasure and own

Beware of these tricksters
Who step with their hipsters

And walk hands-free
Down your local street

Eyeing up your accessory
For today's hot currency

Thou shalt not steal
But it's no big deal

When they're high on hash
And they need some cash

Mothercare

Crutching
Is her skill
Stolen goods to be precise
Sandwiched between two thighs
Concealed by her maternity dress
As she waddles to the checkout
And pays for two baby rompers

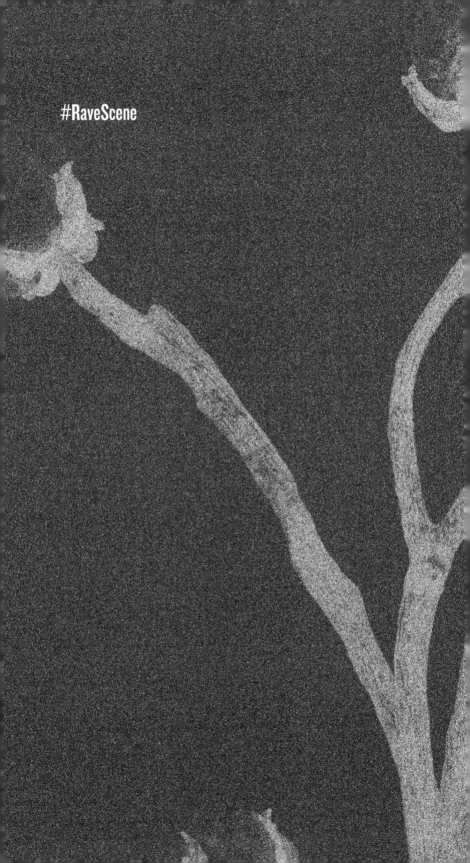
#RaveScene

Yaata's Rap

I have listened to your drum songs, the beat of your feet, the clap of your hands, the bass of your voices. I have watched over your urbanized gatherings in squalid shacks, raising the thatch, ghettoizing the neighbourhoods and attracting flashing sirens. Still, these shebeens, Blues parties and raves created spaces where you could rap your stories and feel safe.

And my children you are drinking the poisons the Hungry Ghosts traded for your lands. You are snorting the coca leaves that your ancestors needed to survive the slog of working in the plantation fields.

These toxins are corrupting and destroying your communities. They are robbing you of your birthright, the sweet territory of silence. Marijuana pyschosis, amphetamines, and opioids induce a disconnection from your inner landscape.

Yes dance, yes sing, and come back to your heart/home, the body. Trust in your inhale and exhale: This will guide you home. Beat your drums, stomp your rhythms. All you need is the soothing breath of my wind: Inhale and exhale. This is the true elixir of life.

People are trapped in history and history is trapped in them.
—JAMES BALDWIN

Essentials for Heaven

iPhone A Flat Screen

Black Mirror Credit Card

A Plastic Note A Wrap A Spliff Doobie BC Bud

DJ Sound System Reggae Hip Hop Trance Techno

Spotify YouTube Apple Music Strobes Zoom

Toilets Cocaine Blade Straw

Afro Comb Hair Extensions Lippy Mascara Shades

Chewing Gum Dance Floor

Go Gos Visuals Projections

Ecstasy Water Dancing Shoes

Poppers Corkscrew Wine Beer

Earplugs Mouth Guard CPAP

Vitamin Pills Echinacea Essential Oils

Twitter Instagram Facebook Messenger

Snapchat WhatsApp Netflix HBO Amazon Prime

Iboga Ayahuasca

Sleeping Pill

Cinders Time

Stones at my window
To tell me
It's Cinderella's time
Midnight

My Princess Charming
Waiting beneath my window
For me to shimmy down
The drainpipe

Tiptoe across the floorboards
To my window
And I give the signal
I flash my cell phone

Five minutes
And I'll be ready
Stuff my bed with
An old blanket

Just in case Mum
Or Dad are paranoid
And do a routine check
On their only daughter

Drag on my baggiest jeans
T-shirt and dancing shoes
Age my face for the night ahead
And down the drainpipe I slide

Stars are bright tonight
My Princess Charming
Shines like the Big Dipper
In the sky

My first night out
At a rave, I'm 25
Borrowed another 10 years
For the event

My Princess has nicked her
Brother's mountain bike
No chariot tonight
Just a hard-battered saddle

Legs almost dead
By the time we reach
The Steamy Gate Way
To Escape from Samsara

Warm gusts gladly greet us
As we join a lineup
Of juvenile delinquents
And ageing hippies

It's 2 a.m. I've been struck by lightning
Great balls of fire
Flashing missiles
Thumping beats make me giddy

I've finally made it into
The cavernous hole
Of Heaven and
Hell

All I want is water
A toilet
Some air
But my Princess
Is in charge
She sits me down
In a corner

Perched on top of a
Mountainous range of
Handbags, coats, shirts
She cavorts around me
Whips me into a frenzy
Fans me with her shirt
Splashes me with
Her water bottle

I'm up like a Jack-in-the-Box
I'm a Jumping Jack

Somersaulting
Between sticky bodies

I subscribe to the aerobic chemistry
Manically bonding with
The frenzied crowd
Crammed in around me

This is Techno
My Princess Charming screams
Tribal Progression, Garage
Trance, Chaos, Freak Out.

I let go of my inhibitions
Hang on to her lyrics
Let myself be hypnotized
By the DJ's pumping beats

Appreciate the mis-education
While secretly wishing that
She will notice I'm exhausted
And all I really want to do

Is go back home
To my warm cozy
Respectable bed
Curl up with my
Winnie-the-Pooh
Hot water bottle
And dance away
In Noddy Land
Where it's
Peaceful
Safe
Still

My First Half

You're staring at this tiny piece of paper
With a dot on it.
And your mate says, *Half or a quarter?*
And you think, *A quarter?*
I want the whole bloody lot.

And then you hesitate
Thinking, *What can this*
Minuscule square piece of paper do?
And your mate says,
If you eat mushrooms,
You can eat this.

And you think, *This ain't organic;*
Mushrooms grow in fields.
You watch your mate
Cut the square into a half
And tweezer it up
Flicking it onto your index finger.

You accept
Gingerly placing it on
The tip of your tongue.
Your mate booms:
Swallow.
And so you swallow
Wondering if this will take you
To the "Dark Side of the Moon."

And then your world begins to swirl
You've lost your mate
And now you're all on your own
Trying to make sense of a rainbow
Catapulting before your eyes.

The next moment you're standing on your head
And everything is sloping up the walls
So you try to sit
But you slide down a wall
Landing on your back.

And the ceiling appears
To be caving in
And you can see every tiny particle
It's made up of.

Your stomach begins to feel queasy
So you crawl to the bathroom
And someone has left their spew.
It smells good.
You begin licking up the food
Realizing this is just what you needed.

The walls begin to collapse
Around you
So you try to swing from a light bulb
But end up falling on top of your mate's body.
You begin making love
And just at the peak of orgasm
You vomit.

But it's okay
Coz your mate says
It's the best ever
Cascading firework display he's ever seen.
But now he wants you to be a rugged waterfall
Running into Scottish waters
So he can be the Loch Ness monster.

He cleans you up.
And you begin to giggle
Almost having a cardiac arrest
And your mate panics.

Somehow you wake up in a strange bed
All on your own.
Eyes peering up to a skylight
And your nearest and dearest
All seem to be flying in
Hovering above your head
And you beg them
To take you
But they laugh and leave you stranded.

You wake up again

This time with your mate at the foot of your bed

Wagging his middle finger

Grinning from ear to ear

Asking: *Are you ready for the next half?*

Class A

A pilot nosedives
Jumbo jets circling my brain
A white powder trail

The chase — smacking out
Brown treacle squirms on foil
Soaring above clouds

Opioids — painless
Sorted — a happy cocktail
A paranoid joint

Dead on the sidewalk
Naloxone wakens my pulse
Alive to this hell

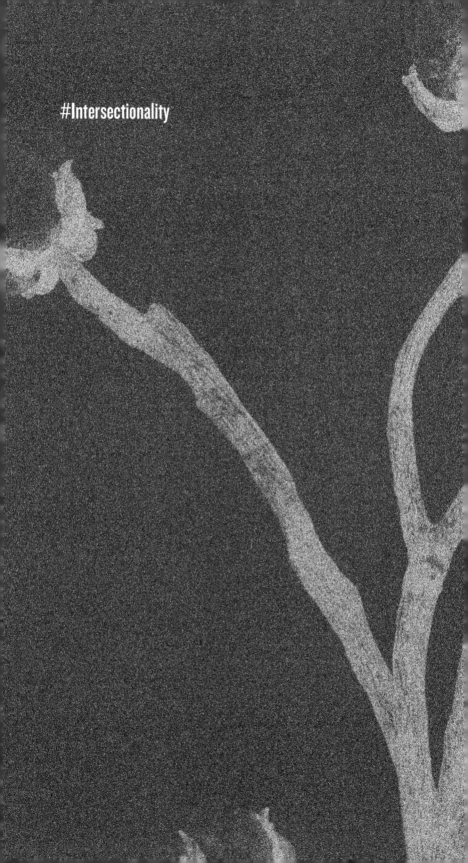
#Intersectionality

Yaata's Prophecy

My progeny have circled life and death. If you listen carefully, you will hear their branches preaching a secret wisdom, see their leaves performing a sacred dance, my birds singing out the truth, my animals roaming in the jungle, my minerals nourishing the earth you live on.

Respect my wealth, my minerals, my earth, my animals and you will bring good fortune to you and your family. Let the ghosts of your past die. No need to slay each other anymore; no need to take your own life. Yaata is everywhere around you.

Breathe again, and live without guns, knives and drugs. Live life, until the body decays, wizens, expires, and bears fruit again in Mother Earth. And you will no longer be victims of your fettered past.

Abolish the labels: Half-Breed, Mulatto, Quadroon, Octoroon. These racist identities have only referred to the mingling of African and white European blood. And loosen your attachments to the label Black. In my continent, you are defined by your character and tribe. You became a colour when you stepped into the colonizers' continents. You are not a commodity; you are the soul and pulse of Mother Earth. It is not necessarily innate that Black folk can run fast, sing and dance well. You ran through my jungles to save your lives. You sang in the plantation fields to pass on your stories. You danced to release your anger and frustration. These identities are adaptation—a result of the passing of epigenetic trauma. Live these personas, but do not be trapped by them.

You once knew how to be still, drum beats were your rituals, and you lived peacefully among the changes of my seasons. And you can be still and peaceful again. You were proud people who walked the land softly and quietly. You sang and danced in ceremony. This wisdom is still in your DNA, and in the Afro-Diaspora. You can summon all of this up in your whole being. Yaata is your backbone, your spine. Let me hold you up, with grace, courage and strength. Yaata still flows through your body.

You have always been home; wherever your body is, you are home. Let nobody take your home away from you with their brutality. Hatred is an illusion, an unwanted gift of delusion from the Hungry Ghosts. Step out of the ignorant projections, constructs and concepts and reclaim your indestructible magnificent bodies.

Love takes off masks that we fear we cannot live without and know we cannot live within.
—JAMES BALDWIN

Self Portrait I
THE COLOUR OF MY SKIN

The colour of my skin is the root of my ecstasy
The seed of my life
The colour of my skin is one of nature's glories
The bloom of my life

The colour of my skin is the flower of my legacy
The taboo of my oppressors
The colour of my skin is the greatness of my splendour
The guilt of my kidnappers

The colour of my skin is the celebration of Eden
Black is an omnipotent being
The rejoicing of life
Black the colour of many skins
Is nature's own deliberation

The colour of my skin is your fear
My strength
Your ignorance
My wisdom
Your blemish
My beauty

Self Portrait 2
CALL ME MY NAME

My Queerness is part of my identity
The love of my chosen families

My Queernesss is nature's resplendence
The flowering of my ancestry

My Queerness is being out of the closet
The karma of my queer-bashers

My Queerness is the emancipation of all beings
A fact of life

Queer, Zami, Adofuro, Yan Daudu, Ikihindu
Our Pride before Colonizers came

Gender Fluid, Non-Binary, Genderqueer, Gender Variant,
Intersex, Agender, Bigender, Transgender, Pangender, Third
Gender, Gender Neutral, Two-Spirit, Mx, Ze, Hir
Is what we reclaim

My Queerness is your fear
My courage

Your exclusion
My embrace

Your shame
My pride

Your fantasy
My reality

Your perception
My revelation

Now say my Name

Man-ifestation

We've been splattered in tabloids
Paraded in shop windows
Modelled in women's weeklies
Flaunted across your screens
Such oppression
Such repression
Our body harbours all this tension

Men have mass-produced us on a conveyor belt
Compartmentalizing our parts
Man-ifesting their perfect woman
Such dictation
Such convention
Our body festers under all these inflictions

I wear a bra to mould a man-made shape
Spanx girdles to hold a man-made shape
If I wear close-fitting clothes men whistle and call me fickle
Their lust brands me a sex object and labels me a slut
Such violation
Such humiliation
Our body breeds all these infections

We are victims of men's perceptions
Spend hours picking spots, pruning brows, shaving legs
Bleaching, perming and straightening our natural hair
Such aggression
Such destruction
Our body riddled with all these man-ifestations

We are slaves to food
Traitors
Martyrs
Secret eaters
Such depression
Such corruption
Our body stewing all this frustration

We are a Barbie narcotic
A walking neurotic
A pill-popping robotic
A media schizophrenic
Such revelations
Such recognition
Our body a man-made creation

A Wake

They howl a song
of death.

Fists thumping heads
With impotence and rage
As they swoop over the coffin
Shrouding the body.

Their child
Dead.

Next of kin take their turn
Furrowed with disbelief
Overwhelmed with grief
Two weeks of wailing.

Their sibling
Dead.

Friends have traversed
A long paranoid path
To pay their last respects
Gifts for the grave.

Their friend
Dead.

And now
It's time to wail
Again the song of death
As dust and soil
Shroud this man.

The final epitaph
Another Black man
Dead.

Forget and Pretend

Is it strength, anger or desperation?
Perhaps all are woven into the insanity of life.
Born to die.
Born to die.

Relatives, lovers, friends, enemies
All clamped to the wheel of living.
Struggle and strife.
Struggle and strife.

Her death, his death, their death
Claimed by suicide.
Fate and fortune.
Fate and fortune.

Suicide and we are left with the guilt.
Suicide and we are left with the pain.
Suicide and we are left with the anger.

Their anger, their pain, their guilt
Drove them to suicide.
Living is suicide.
Suicide is living.

No time to grieve.
No time to mourn
The death of our friends
As we must put it behind us.

Forget and Pretend.
Forget and Pretend.

Again Becoming

Winter is barren
My spirit withers once more
Incarcerated

Spring buds sprout again
Like another pregnancy
A granddaughter born

Summer boasts her rays
Radiant — promising life
But potent like death

Autumn leaves drop down
Decaying on my tombstone
Again Becoming

Farewell My Fiend

The time has come
To say farewell my fiend
Who has feasted upon my heart
Haunted my thoughts
Weighing me down
With stories that have racialized my mind

The time has come
To make peace with my vampire
Who has leeched life from my heart
Deranged my thoughts
Drunk me dry
And festered in the prisms of my mind

The time has come
To begin living in the now
And let my nemesis die
First, I will tell it thank you
There is no room for you anymore
Second, I will cut the umbilical cord
And with compassion let it go, let it go, let it go

Yaata's Epilogue

My people, everything you have done and continue to do has not allowed you to be free. Your liberation has been stifled by the narratives that have been foisted upon you by the Hungry Ghosts. These stories have become your assaulted truth. Interrupt the Hungry Ghosts' delusions with your self-love and love for one another. Your mere presence will become potent. It will disturb the underbelly of white domination, and threaten the atrocious views of your Black and Brown bodies.

My blood will always return. I dwell in every continent. I, Yaata, will not sleep peacefully until the ravaging of my earth stops and the necessary reparations are made. Until the colonizers apologize to my people. I will not sleep until my people are no longer executed in the streets, no longer cooped up in institutions, and no longer objects of the white gaze. I, Yaata, will never forget. I will remember and forgive, and love all sentient beings. Yaata harkens to the cries of all suffering. Those who have been slaves, and those who have enslaved. I am the mother of all beings.

Remember, humankind began in Africa with Lucy and every one of you descend from me. Yes! Lucy is the ancestor of every race in the world. And all of you must someday find peace.

You have to decide who you are and force the world to deal with you, not with its idea of you.
    —*JAMES BALDWIN*

Acknowledgements

I give thanks to the Ancestors who have moved through me to share social justice poetic narratives on these pages. To the father, grandfathers and grandmothers I have never known, who walk beside me on this earth, thank you for embodying me to share some of your stories.

I thank all those who have walked before me and made it possible for me to be here today and live as a Black person in the West with the freedoms they never had. I stand tall on your shoulders and continue the work of bringing harmony and healing to a generation of people who have been traumatized by the legacies of slavery.

"The Villain" and "The Binge" were published in Mother Tongues (Literary Exchange Press, 2003). "Yellowknife" was published in *The Great Black North: Contemporary African Canadian Poetry* (Frontenac House, 2013); "The Windrush" and "The Colour of My Skin" were published in *Brown Girl in the Ring* (Get a Grip, 1999).

For those interested in learning more about Willimae Moore's 1955 trial referenced in "Yellowknife," I recommend Constance Backhouse's *Carnal Crimes: Sexual Assault Law in Canada, 1900–1975* (Toronto: Irwin Law, 2008).

Thank you to Micheline Maylor who gave me the confidence to listen to my ancestors. Thank you to Jannie Edwards, my editor and proofreader, for her excitement, passion and critical eye as she read each piece on these pages. Thank you to Mary Lou Roy for her attention to detail. It was a blessing.

Thank you to Peter Midgley for a being a fan of my written words, and to University of Alberta Press for having the courage and boldness to publish *I Am Still Your Negro: An Homage to James Baldwin*.

Thank you to Michelle McKenzie and Jo Fraser for being my language consultants. And thank you also to my kindred spirit, my partner Che Kehoe, for supporting me in all the work that I do.

Thank you to all the people I have ever known. We are interconnected, and I could not have produced this piece of poetic art without your friendships, encouragement, and inspiration.

Other Titles from University of Alberta Press

An Autobiography of the Autobiography of Reading

DIONNE BRAND

How Black life is made and unmade by and in
literature; arguing for new vocabularies.

CLC *Kreisel Lecture Series*

100 Days

JULIANE OKOT BITEK

Poems that recall the senseless loss of life and of
innocence in Rwanda.

Robert Kroetsch Series

Dear Sir, I Intend to Burn Your Book

An Anatomy of a Book Burning

LAWRENCE HILL

Threat of book burning ignites passionate
discussion about censoring, banning, and other
responses to books.

Henry Kreisel Memorial Lecture Series

More information at uap.ualberta.ca